© Sheila Maxey

MAKEPOVERTY**HIST**… all those people in B… right prevail'. It is a y… our Prime Minister ch… of the eight richest cou…ies in the world – and when Britain takes over the presidency of the European Union, one of the most powerful economic groupings in the world. Thank God we live in a country where we are free to write protest letters, to lobby, to demonstrate, to make our voices heard in season and out of season.

The **MAKE**POVERTY**HISTORY** campaign is a unique UK alliance of charities, trade unions, campaigning groups, faith communities and celebrities who are mobilising around key opportunities in 2005 to drive forward the struggle against poverty and injustice. The United Reformed Church and, of course, Christian Aid are committed members of this alliance. It is campaigning for a three-pronged practical and achievable attack on world poverty:

1.   Trade justice – allowing fragile economies to
        protect their goods
2.   Drop the debt – for the poorest countries
3.   More and better aid.

All of us have a part to play. The United Reformed Church has always been at the heart of such campaigns – Jubilee 2000, Fair Trade and many more. Many members quietly and persistently write letters, shop responsibly, support with money and prayers. However 2005 offers particular opportunities to influence the 'make-it-happen' people. This extra effort to defeat world poverty needs to be fed spiritually, emotionally and intellectually. This small book seeks to do just that. There are key statements and information, stories and poems, dramatic readings and prayers. The United Reformed Church offers this book as a contribution to the **MAKE**POVERTY**HISTORY** campaign in the hope it will inspire and encourage all those who 'hunger and thirst to see right prevail.'

© Sheila Maxey
Moderator, General Assembly of the United Reformed Church

Overcoming poverty is not a gesture of charity. It is an act of justice.

Nelson Mandela

2005 is a year of opportunity. If every one who wants to see an end to poverty, hunger and suffering speaks out, then the noise will be deafening. Politicians will have to listen.

Archbishop Desmond Tutu

The United Nations estimates that poor countries are denied $700 billion because of unfair trade rules.

Christian Aid

2005 is our chance to go down in history for what we did do, rather than what we didn't do.

Bono

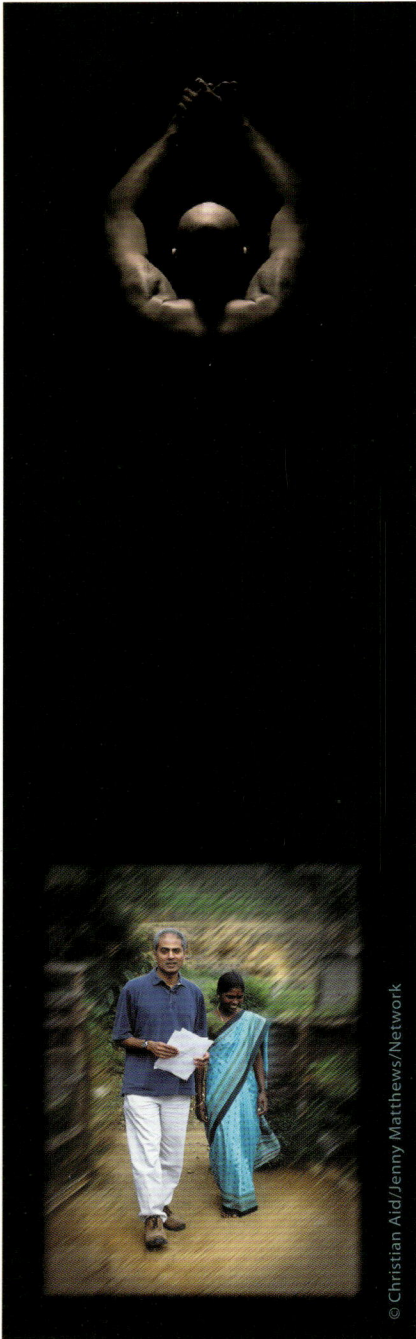

© Christian Aid/Jenny Matthews/Network

George Alagiah and Engel Selvi a tea-picker from Sri Lanka

Engel Selvi is fighting for better conditions for women tea-pickers in the face of intense discrimination. She's the leader of a women's group run by the Christian Aid-supported Institute for Social Development. 'We're learning to fight back, to assert the rights of women,' she told the BBC's George Alagiah. 'We're no longer taking "no" for an answer.'

What a Way to Earn a Living

On the coast of Ghana sit two 'castles', prisons for many millions of Africans who were captured into slavery in past centuries – 15 million transported to the Americas. It was on this trade in humans as commodities that wealth in Europe was built. Over the cells where the slaves were imprisoned waiting for deportation, was a chapel. Christians worshipped God while directly below, right under their feet, those being sold into slavery languished in chains and in horror of those dungeons.

(adapted from a message to the Churches,
World Alliance of Reformed Churches Council in Accra 2004.)

From the brilliant African light
deep into these dark filthy cells
we crowd together retching from the stench of naked flesh against flesh,
tightly packed, containers of trade for overseas.
One on top of another, gasping for the free air of our homeland.
We stare at the grill above
as shards of blistering light
shear our black faces.
We see the dancing feet
and hear the stranger's strange songs.

Out from the burning intensity of African heat
to our cool chapel to sing praises to God.
This dark and filthy land
with its fearsome black dogs
causes us to sing the psalms of release and
freedom.
The animals underneath our feet,
rescued from their alien land,
will give us a little wealth and reward.
We look down at those white startled eyes
repelled by their hoary breath.

Who might these strangers be
who have brought us here?
What will they do to us –
Offer us up for sacrifice to their gods?

Who might these animals be
Who have brought us here?
What will they do to us
– if they ever escape –
offer us up to their primitive gods?

God – save us from this place.
Lord, out of the depths I have called to you.

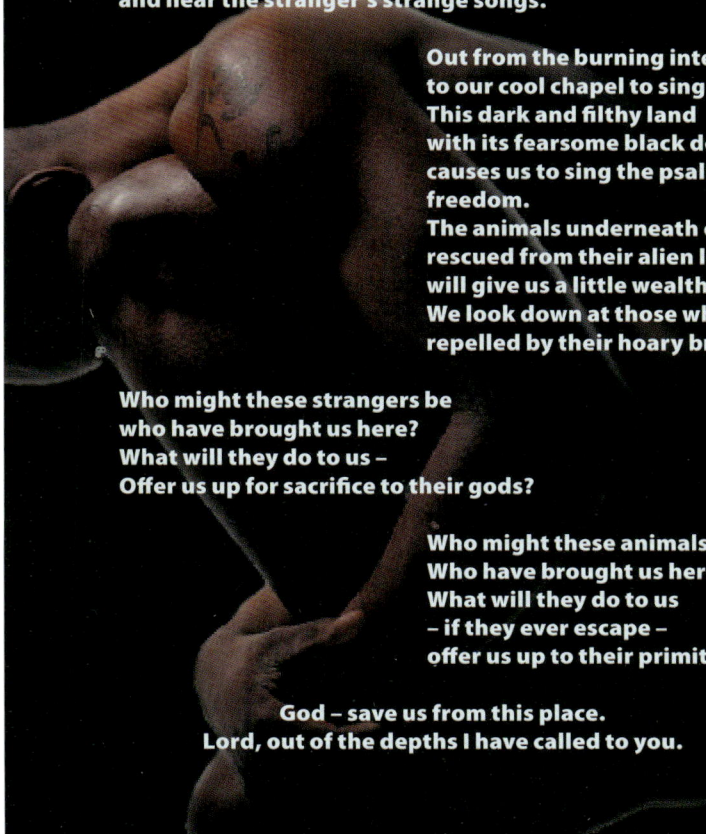

© Martin Hazell

The Slavery of Free Trade

Kofi from Ghana is a victim of free trade. He earns £1.00 a day breaking rocks to make gravel. He used to be a tomato farmer but that livelihood which brought food for his family and schooling for his children has been taken away from him.

Free trade means a country's economy is run without government intervention. It is a policy that rich country governments and international institutions are forcing poor countries to accept.

Voices from India

Voice 1　　Voices crying in the wilderness.

　　　　　　Every visitor to the dried out lands of our world will be determined to challenge the structures that allow so many to live and die in poverty. These stories present just a small sketch of some of the hardships people in South India face every day of their lives.

　　　　　　Let's hear first from Amala:

Wishing She Could Rear Goats

Voice 2　'Only 30 rupees'

Voice 1　 – that's 40 pence to us –

Voice 2　'Only 30 rupees – that's what I get a day breaking up granite – it's hard work, and tedious. And dangerous – a friend was chipping granite when a piece flew into her eye. There was no medical help and now she is blind.

I would much rather look after goats but there is no money to buy a herd so that we – me and the other women – can rear goats and sell them to get extra money

Perhaps, in time, we could gang together and set up a Credit Union and charge less interest than the banks'.

Voice 1　This young woman, Amala, lives in the drought stricken area in the north of Karnataka State, south India.

Voice 1   Now, Mudamma, is just nineteen.

Mudamma

Voice 3   'Festival times are good for business – I can at least make sarees to sell to the other women in the village. But most of the year we have to rely on growing crops. The land is parched – we just can't grow enough crops to feed the whole family, my mother included, and have enough over to sell at the local market. My husband has to go away to Pune or Mumbai to try and earn a living as a migrant worker. Most times he returns with nothing – there is no work to be had. We have a young daughter to care for – what future for her?'

Voice 1   Mudamma has polio. She lives in a very remote community in south India. She lives in a small house which is shared with a dog, a chicken and a cow and is in a very poor state of repair caused by weather conditions and age.

This is a common image, a man working a pump:

Unable to Irrigate the Land

Voice 4   'I peddle away all day just to get a trickle of water to water my land. I only have a small area of land to grow crops for food for the family and for sale in the local community. Water is in such short supply. I have to bring it up from a nearby well to irrigate the land. There is never enough for the whole of my tiny plot.

Year in year, my crops fail.'

Voice 1   This man lives five hundred kilometres away from where rich tourists swim in their hotel pools.

Voices crying in the wilderness – waiting and hoping that poverty will become history.

Text and pictures © Geoffrey Duncan
adapted by Martin Hazell

Consuming Passions

Do we consume goods
or do our goods consume us?

Generous God,
we thank you for the riches you offer us:
provisions for the body, provisions for the soul –
enough, and more, for all your creatures!
Forgive us our discontent – our passion
for 'more', 'bigger', 'latest', 'best' –
which means that for others there will be
'less', 'smallest', outdated' , even 'useless' …
Forgive us the passion to consume –
for voices that persuade, hearts that envy,
eyes that long, hands that seize …
Forgive us our obsession with ownership and power.
Spent and risen Christ,
whose consuming passions are love and justice
and the unseen treasures of the soul,
teach us again about the values that endure:
help us to appreciate
voices that count the cost of greed,
hearts that go out to the exploited,
eyes that can see a new and fairer path,
and hands that reach out in generous sharing.
Help us to simplify our lives;
and remind us that your power
lies in dispossession and service to others.

Energizing Spirit,
mysterious Wind of Change,
blow through our world and our lives.
Give us a consuming passion
to speak with the voice of the prophet,
to campaign with hearts of enthusiasm,
to see with the eyes of visionaries,
and to act with the hands of artists –
fashioning new and fairer societies,
where trade is shaped by the love of neighbour
rather than the love of profit,
and where justice shines among the nations.

Mind the Gap

(A meditation based on Luke 16:19-31)

He doesn't think about me seeing him
(and pretends he doesn't see me).
Natty dresser, overfed, jowled,
careful not to let even the hem of his cashmere coat
touch the running sores that cover every inch of my body.

For years I worked at his factory, stitching footballs,
barely making enough to feed my family.

It was the work of my hands that has made him fat and rich.
Across the ocean, people pay what is several months' wages to me
to see leather, stuffed and sewn by me,
kicked about by young men with more money still.

No one sees me.
No one sees that, without me, there is no game.

The preacher tells me my day will come … on the other side.
But the cries of hungry children stop up my ears.
I cannot believe that God blesses this state of affairs.

He doesn't think about me seeing him
(and pretends not to see me).
Averts his eyes, sweeps his coat to the side.
But I know he knows.
I know he knows my name and he knows my need.
Knows it well enough to know that I will do what he asks,
if it will give me daily bread and milk for the baby.
He'll know it even on the other side,
where he will dare to ask for cool comfort from my fingertips,
where he would will me to life for a word of warning to his brothers.
Always a tool, a thing, to be used,
that is what I am to him.
This is the great chasm,
fixed by his refusal
to see and to know
I am who I am.

I see him, better than he sees himself.

God sees all.

Today, I Cheated A Little Girl

Dear Jesus,

Today I cheated a little girl out of the football she had made for me.

I took a new pair of trainers from a boy who owns no shoes.

I haggled with the father of ten children over the price of a cup of coffee.

It was so easy.

It was easy to cheat the girl; she was so poor.

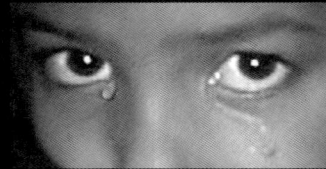

Easy to trick the boy; he had no friends.

Easy to beat that father down; his children were so hungry.

Poor, helpless, hungry; I was beating you down too.

I am part of that crooked world.

Help me go straight, Jesus.

Honest Jesus, help me be straight.

Amen.

© Lucy Berry

Fairtrade

Supermarkets are an effective way to launch new ideas for the consumer. The church where I am a member sent a letter to the local Tesco branch to highlight **Fairtrade** fortnight in March 2002:

March 2002: ... '**Fairtrade** is about people who deserve a decent livelihood .... Consumers, can make the world fairer for people by buying products with the **Fairtrade** mark. It is the policy adopted by the trader which governs whether we find the **Fairtrade** marked goods .... We ask that the **Fairtrade** marked provisions you already stock and those we hope you will stock for the future, be boldly identified ... and placed where easily found. I hope you will find it possible to expand this market and would be grateful to receive your comments.'

Reply from Tesco said it was important for them to hear from customers as comments and suggestions helped them to decide which policies to follow and which products to sell. My letter was being forwarded to their local Customer Service Department.

July, 2003: I had not received any information from the local Customer Service Department, so I obtained the name of the Manager and wrote directly to him. No reply. I made another direct approach by telephone and was told that replies were not sent to letters regarding their policy on what provisions were stocked. After further telephone enquiries I wrote to the Customer Service Manager at the head office. In October 2003 I received a letter which stated they were concerned to learn of my complaint and the inconvenience caused. It continued *'The relevant department dealing with such matters has been notified and I can assure you that this will be taken on board at the next review meeting. I cannot guarantee that action will be taken, however, your views and comments are invaluable to us.'*

November 2003: I wrote again *' … you gave no indication when the review meeting would take place or if you would inform me of the decision. … I am sure you will understand my interpretation of your letter, as saying nothing would be done. … It is difficult to understand why such a big issue is being made of this request. All it takes is a placard saying, for example,* **Fairtrade** *Bananas'. Placards are hung above the shelves showing 'Loose Bananas', 'Special Value Bananas'…Why is there is aversion to highlighting* **Fairtrade** *bananas?' This would be a great boost for the Tesco image … I have been patiently awaiting an active response since my initial letter to you in March 2002.'*

Reply received five days later:…*'I would like to assure you that I have recorded your views and will pass them on, together with any others we may receive, for the consideration of our Marketing Department.'*

I responded to the letter with a telephone call to the Customer Service Manager, only to be told she had left the employ of Tesco. I was advised that the decisions of the 'Review Body' are never communicated to those who write in with suggestions.

November 2004: I wrote again to Tesco, addressing my letter to the manager of the local store.

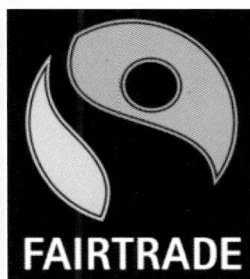

FAIRTRADE

November 2004… *'***Fairtrade Goods*** … Today I wished to buy biscuits and looked carefully along the shelves but could not find any* **Fairtrade** *packets. I asked at the customer reception for both biscuits and cakes to be told that you did not stock either commodity. The person on the desk had no idea to what I was referring, until I explained the ethics of paying a living wage to the people who produce these goods. I know that no action is taken on a request such as mine, my previous experience with you makes this quite clear. But I could not let this go without informing you. I shall endeavour to use either the Co-op or Sainsbury's in the future, with occasional shopping at Tesco to see if* **Fairtrade** *has been emphasised in your store. I regret this decision and I know it will not affect your profits or indeed concern you unduly. I am so disappointed in the Tesco policy on this.*

I shall continue to write, and to enquire not only of Tesco, but of other stores where I shop. Let us remember that 'constant dripping, wears away the hardest stone'. YOU can make a difference.

A 'geldof' Moment

Open your eyes.
Open your ears.
Open your hearts.
Open your bloody hands.

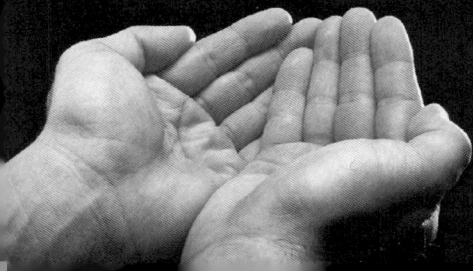

Give up your power.
Give up your subsidies.
Write off the debts.
Give us some bloody help.

Out with the tyrants.
Out with war.
Out with the expensive medicines.
Out with self-serving politicians.

Give us some bloody help.

The cry of the poor
is often never heard
above the roar of self-satisfaction
from the rich.
They cry – 'give us help'
and the rich give what the rich think good.
Let us be free ...
of debt;
of disease;
of hate;
of hunger and thirst.
Share for the sake of your soul if not our lives.

Share for the sake of all the people on earth
so we all can have a bloody chance.

Open your bloody hands.

A Litany for the Money-givers

Voice One: It's time to give.
All: **So we give what we can.**

Voice One: It's time to give because the need is great.
All: **So we give what we can to meet the need.**

Voice One: It's time to give because the need is great and the aid will help.
All: **So we give what we can to meet the need**
and make things a little better.

Voice One: It's time to give because the need is great and the aid will help.
Voice Two: Is it still only the time to give our money?
All: **So we give what we can to meet the need**
and make things a little better
and yet we worry and wonder.

Voice One: It's time to give because the need is great and the aid will help.
Voice Two: What if God demands more from us than just a bit of our wealth?
All: **So we give what we can to meet the need**
and make things a little better
and we open our Bibles to hear God teach
that charity must not replace justice.

Voice One: It's time to give because the need is great and the aid will help.
Voice Two: It's time to do much more than give
for aid will not right the wrongs that keep millions poor.
All: **So we give what we can**
and let our giving be only the beginning.

Voice One: It's time to give because the need is great and the aid will help.
Voice Two: It's time to agitate because the need is great
and our voices must protest.
All: **So we give what we can and we write what we can**
and we settle ourselves to lives of bold opposition
to all that enslaves a world in poverty.

Voice One: It's time to be Christians for the poor.
Voice Two: It's time to be Christians for the poor.
All: **It's time to be Christians for the poor.**

Trade Justice?

Trade Justice?
I do my best
I buy   CaféDirect
        fair trade chocolate
        recycled loo-rolls
        low-energy lightbulbs
Oh no, wait,
that's something else …
But anyway,
I do my best
but it all feels too big
and I don't understand
tariffs and subsidies
exports and surpluses …
What does it mean?
      I am struggling.

Trade Justice?
What does it mean?
I used to work
I made shoes in the factory
all the village men did
and our children were fed
but the factory closed
now we buy foreign shoes.
But no, wait, that's not right:
we have no wage
to buy shoes or clothes
or even good food …
and I don't understand
tariffs and subsidies
exports and surpluses …
What does it mean?
I am suffering.

God of justice and truth,
when we struggle to understand
the complex questions of our day,
when we find ourselves confused
by distortions of truth
when we feel powerless
in the face of injustice,
help us
to listen to each other
to tell our stories
to everyone who will listen
and to the powerful people
who don't want to hear.
Show us how to use our freedom
not to forge the chains of others
but to set one another free.

© Heather Pencavel

A Hymn for Trade Justice

God, whose people cry with yearning
For the lifting of debt's strain,
Give to us the will for turning
From our ruthless search for gain.
Keep us struggling,
Keep us faithful,
In the fight to heal earth's pain.

God, who made the earth for sharing
Help us work for fairer trade.
In our affluent lack of caring
Help us see the price we've paid.
Grant repentance,
Grant forgiveness,
For the unjust world we've made.

God, whose holy anger fires us,
Make your cry for justice heard.
Light the vision that inspires us,
Challenge with prophetic word.
Make us restless,
Make us angry,
For the changing of your world.

God, embracing all creation,
Bringing life and hope to birth,
Give to every human nation
A true sense of what life's worth.
Give us freedom,
Give us wisdom,
For the saving of the earth.

Tune: Rhuddlan

© Jan Berry

I.O.U.

Lord, I ... owe ... you ... my life. I owe you my daily bread.
I owe you the roof over my head, my shoes and my bed,
My going out and coming in.
I owe you the people I love, my joy and my purpose.

You gave us more than we can ever give back.
And you never ask.

The only way we can honour our endless debt to you
is to copy you: to forgive our debtors as you forgive our debts.

But we don't do that.

The endless IOU's which we hold against our poorest neighbours,
were borrowed in desperation, to avoid ruin. Like our debts to you,
these are debts that can never be paid back.

They owe us everything they have.
You gave us everything we have.

Let's tear up all the IOU's and redeem ourselves,
expecting nothing back – except all the joy and celebration.

And the knowing that we are being like you.

© Lucy Berry

Kwame Kwei-Armah visited a Christian Aid partner, the African Network for Integrated Development (RADI).

'Before I went to Senegal, I didn't really understand how grossly unfair international trade has become and how the losers are the poorest people in the world's least-developed countries, ' explained Kwame Kwei-Armah. 'I saw a very proud people, ultimately fighting a losing battle because of policies made in rich countries.'

I Am Very Small

Loving God,
I am very small
and I am only one:
what can I do
to change the hearts of governments,
banks and multi-nationals,
and influence the many and the powerful,
so as to make poverty history?

Brother Christ,
you have valued me
and given me allies and friends.
Together we can do much:
we can show the effects of 'free' trade
and the debt burden,
by writing, singing, speaking, campaigning:
we can envision a new world!

Go-between Spirit,
goad me today
into adding my small candle-flame
to all whose lives burn for justice,
that we may set the world on fire!
Together, may we defeat cynicism,
selfishness and greed,
and be parables of caring, sharing
and generosity.

© Kate Compston

Dawn French gives her support to **Make**Poverty**History** and their three points:

- ♦ **Debt Cancellation**
- ♦ **Trade Justice**
- ♦ **More and better aid for poor countries**

Dawn French walked with women priests from St Martin-in-the Fields, London to 10 Downing Street showing solidarity with **Make**Poverty**History**

© Bob Allen

Wear a white band, the symbol of the **Make**Poverty**History** campaign. The White band is about sending a message that you want poverty to be stopped.

Wear it how and where you like.

Ten years ago, poor countries' export sales of coffee were worth a third of the total coffee market. Today, it is just 10%. Coffee farmers are getting, on average, $1 a kilogram while consumers in rich countries are paying roughly $15 a kilogram – a mark up of 1500%.

© Oxfam

Poor God

'The poor are always with us'

Yes, they are!
Help us to look each other in the face,
as we wait in endless queues,
and struggle to pay the bills.

'The poor are always with us'

Yes, they are!
Help us to speak out when the cold wind bites,
when the economic prospects are bleak,
when 'the cost of recession is a few job losses up north'[1].

'The poor are always with us'

Yes, they are!
Help us to act justly when we have the power,
to put our money where our mouths are,
to put our skills to better use.

'The poor are always with us'

Yes, they are!
Together may we wait with each other,
find our voices to speak out and act for justice
in ways that push poverty out of our communities,
puts an end to ghettos and gives us the will to live on.

[1]   *Eddie George, then governor of the*
     Bank of England, said this in November 1998

Water Justice

Years ago when visiting El Salvador I met with parents in a Christian base community whose son had disappeared. Four days later his tortured body was found in a city garbage heap. His crime was to run two miles of piping from a clean water source to his squatters community. One tap served the community and ended the several four mile long trips a day needed to provide clean water. The people who killed him also ripped up the pipes.

Water is about self-determination and control.

In Angola, civil war had driven people from the regions to the capital Luanda. In the townships now surrounding the city, most people live without running water. Since the war officially ended things have improved but life is still difficult. The government ships water into the city by tanker truck which is then poured into collection areas where I watched children gather with large containers. They filled their containers and carried the water home on their hips and heads several times a day for drinking, cooking and bathing.

Water is about health and war.

One thing you learn when visiting Palestine is that Israel controls the use of water. Since 1967 Israel has allocated fixed water quotas for the Occupied Territories. Palestinians have been forbidden to dig wells for agricultural use. The barrier now being built by Israel separates some Palestinian communities and farms from their water sources. In the Territories agriculture provides employment for 15% in the West Bank and 17% in the Gaza Strip. 30% of water used by households in Tel Aviv comes from the West Bank. Less than a dozen wells for Palestinian domestic use have been allowed. In Gaza where 5000 settlers live in the midst of 1,325,000 Palestinians, the Israeli government appropriates up to 25% of Gaza water for the settlers. All Palestinians pay a minimum of 15% more for their water than Israelis and Jewish settlers. From the CIA World Factbook the following are listed as current environmental issues: desertification;
        salination of fresh water;
                sewage treatment;
                        water-borne disease;
                                soil degradation;
                                        depletion and contamination of
                                        underground water resources.

Water is about food, employment, justice, and survival.

Without clean water there is poverty and poor health.
Over one billion people lack safe water to drink and to use for sanitation.
Without water there can be no self-determination and there is less employment.
Without the wise use of water there is environmental degradation.
Without the sharing of water there will be no security and peace.
Individuals and communities can have no life without water.
Water justice is simply necessary.

Tap Dancing

Fresh sparkling water flows through the garden turning all to a lush,
green pasture ...
Precious water, life-giving water, free-to-all water ...

A tap is turned

The flow is stopped and the hand that turns holds the power
reversing the garden to a barren desert.
Creation becomes uncreation
water and food withdrawn at once.

The dancing children stall and turn,
their eyes of laughter sink into their cheeks,
fit to burst,
begging for life.

Water, flowing and pure, against water, stagnant and diseased.
So easily, at a turn of a tap.
Life and death, unhappy neighbours, sit side by side.
How is this justice?
... Those who have ...
... Those who have not ...
The spring of life is extinguished with the turn of a tap.

Tap, tap, tap.

And the political dance goes on.

The turn of a tap

And life can flow again. Justice at last, essentials for all. So easy, so easy.

We are the brothers and sisters of our world,
sitting side by side,
children who may dance in the rainbow of water and light.
Hope for the world.

Let Justice Flow

**Let justice flow on like a river and righteousness
like a never-failing torrent
(Amos 5:24)**

As the stream tumbles
over rocks and through brambles,
I think of God's justice,
flowing forever.

As the reservoirs empty,
exposing the bare earth,
I think of God's justice,
that never runs dry.

As the storm clouds gather,
piling up thunder in the sky
I yearn for God's justice
to drench me again.

As the floods carry away
the lives of my neighbours
I wonder about God's justice,
keeping the rice pot afloat.

As the hurricane roars
peeling back roofs, exposing inside,
I wonder about God's justice,
uprooting palm trees.

As the drizzle lingers,
the moors veiled in clouds,
I wonder about God's justice,
bathing me impartially.

**We wonder about your justice,
God of all integrity.
We hunger for it to flow,
to sweep away unjust laws and practices.
We yearn for it to fill us up,
to swell our half-hearted attempts at fair trade
and ethical investment.
Worried by rates and taxes,
troubled by reports of global warming,
we struggle to share even an umbrella
as soft rain falls.
Flow on, just God.
carry us to that ocean of righteousness,
that springs up eternally.**

© Janet Lees

Note: the first six stanzas can
be spoken by different voices.

Unacceptable ... Obscene

Leader: Living Lord, thank you for the opportunity to know about suffering caused by poverty like ...

The two year old girl who sleeps on the pavement of a Tanzanian city.

All: **Forgive us as we watch the television and give only a passing thought to her suffering.**

Leader: This two year old girl had her toes eaten away by rats as she slept.

All: **Forgive us as we watch the television and feel revulsion because our sensitivities are damaged.**

Leader: This precious two year old girl is unable to walk.

All: **Forgive us as we watch the television and get on with our lives.**

Leader: Living Lord make us more aware of the results of poverty.

All: **Please give our senses a jolt ... so that we know it is unacceptable for a two year old child to be subjected to this obscenity:**

Leader: One child dies every 15 seconds because of pollutec water.

One child dies every 30 seconds from malaria.

4,000 women, men and children die each day from HIV/AIDS.

30,000 children die each day because of poverty.

Living Lord make us even more aware of the results of poverty.

All: **Please help us to realise that it is unacceptable for children and adults to live in the death-shadows caused by poverty and the inhumanity of rich nations.**

Leader: Give us the courage to take action for these poor and suffering people as we:

All: **Stand up**

Leader: Make our feet walk

All:	**Speak out**
Leader:	Make our voices heard
All:	**To employers, multi-national directors and governments who need to know practical compassion**
Leader:	And may all people know justice and peace in their lives for no, not God's sake nor for the sake of our Lord Jesus Christ but for the sake of humankind spurred on by our Loving God … Compassionate Christ … Justice-filled Spirit.

Amen

Give Me the Courage to Speak Out

Forgive me Lord for my part in the mess
that the world's now in,
for the ways in which I've searched for a bargain
and switched off the news when it's touched a nerve.

Remind me of the woman pounding maize outside
her mud-brick home, the one who aspires
to buy clothes as nice as mine
and soap to wash her baby.

Next time I am blaming governments
and world leaders, tell it to me straight,
how my inaction leaves the poor paralysed
and my words not worthy.

Fill me with a hunger for justice,
courage to speak out when I want to blend in.
Make me passionate for the needs of the neighbour
I do not know.
Move me.
Move me.
Move me on.

Making it Happen

Extracts from an article written for the
Christian Socialist Movement Journal

© News International

The Rt Hon Hilary Benn, Secretary of State for International
Development, looks at the role the UK can play in leading
the fight against poverty in 2005.

- The UK intends to make 2005 a year of opportunity for the
  world's poorest people.
- The UK will be at the forefront of the fight since in 2005 we
  hold the Presidency of both the G8 and the European Union.

The UK has four priorities for tackling poverty in 2005

- We need more aid and to improve its effectiveness
- We need to create a global trading system that is fair to all
- The burden of developing countries' debts stops them investing in helping poor people
  … too many poor countries are still having to spend money paying off old debts when
  that money would be better used to meet real needs in providing schools and hospitals
- The international commitment needs to continue to be matched by the commitment
  of developing country governments themselves – to develop their own plans to beat
  poverty … aid works best when we're helping poor countries to help themselves.

Here I Am

Here I am,
once
your voice called me
to speak out for justice and peace.
I protested against
the compromise and corruption
of elders and ministers
of church and country.

Here I am,
again
now your voice calls
for justice and peace
and protests against
the complacency and comfort
of me and my generation
of church and country.

How can I pray and protest
for justice and peace
and not break into my bank balance
to the point of sacrifice?
How can I pray and protest
for trade justice
and not change my consumer choices?
How can I pray and protest
to make poverty history
and not practice fasting?

Help me to hear your voice calling
and help me to respond in simple obedience.

In the name and Spirit
of Jesus Christ my Saviour.
Amen.

© Terry Oakley

By the Grace of God?

I eat, drink, learn, have shelter, go to the doctor.
Do I grumble? Yes, but I am lucky. Is that what I feel?

I hear reports of thousands without food, without water, stories of the
HIV/ AIDS pandemic, economic bullying by wealthy countries of those in
debt, sometimes they feel like rumours.

Is this God's grace to me?

Even to whisper that to myself is blasphemy.

God withholding grace from THEM?

I'm lucky.
It isn't the grace of God. I am lucky.

It isn't true that God has no grace for them, that the creator of the heavens
and earth, in whose image all are made, and to whom each is precious
has made division between those like me who have so much and the
many here, there, everywhere who barely have strength to move and
whose hope is in surviving one more day.

God gazes in judgement through the anguished children and despairing
adults. God weeps as Jesus wept over Jerusalem. God is angry.

Such a travesty, a ghastly miserable tragedy that need not be. There's
plenty, knowledge and skills are great, medicine can be made, food can
be shared and this is the purpose and plan of creation, whose groan
echoes in the hopeless places, in the misery of lives begun and ended in
the servitude of poverty.

It is the grace of God that we can pray and act to be the instruments of
hope, of justice with peace. Not just to hear rumours, but to plant hope in
the name and for the sake of Jesus weeping as he embraces them, too.

Yes, I'm lucky, I eat, drink, learn, have shelter, go to the doctor.
But more than luck, by the grace of God, this I can do . . .

© John Ll Humphreys

Remember Tsunami?
Remember the Unremembered?

A wave of horror, destruction
no early warning, no money.
So many killed, wounded
damaged life, destroyed families
shattered communities.
Waves of sickness, physical, emotional scars deeply wounding
Colossal.

In its wake too, nation competing with nation
demonstrating solidarity, making pledges,
delivering as we should?
And another huge wave – this time giving, genuine concern and compassion.
Humanity's divine spirit released across the globe, reaching out.
I, too, will do something.
Tsunami waves of solidarity, donations flowed, rivers of justice.
As they should.

But why? Why this compassion because of tsunami. Why such media coverage?
Was Christmas such a quiet period for 'news'?
Tragic, awful, horrific.
The earthquake, waves of water, pain to individuals, even to Europeans –
one of those disaster movies come to life, or death.

The powerless victims of nature's raw power need our friendship.
And, always there is such devastation and misery and pain.
Children weep as mothers, fathers, siblings die
for the lack of medicine to treat people with HIV/ AIDS.
Mothers watch children die for lack of food and safe water.
Governments struggling to repay interest on debts to us can't resource schools
educate their people, or resource development to empower their people.
Island communities drown from global warming,
our decisions to pollute and the slowness of the drowning helps us ignore.
The unrelenting constancy of poverty creates no splash to shock our comfort.
There's no wave or drama.
How little the constancy of damaged lives reaches our hearts and pockets.

Can waves of compassion roll on with no tsunami?

They can, we can, and governments can!

Making Waves

I

Silence
extends everywhere.
After the roar
the crash
and the chaos,
there is only silence
Words
were sucked out to sea
and have not yet returned.

II

For billions and billions of years,
God has kept company
with God's self
in silence.
A niner may be enough
to wobble the earth,
but in the span of eternity,
where worlds spin on and on,
silence is the biggest thing
in the universe and
the only One that can
embrace us all.

III

Making waves
is what we must all do now:
across continents,
through the EU and the G8
and beyond.
Where bloated bodies were piled high
and matchsticks all that was left
of whole communities,
rebuilding will require more than
truck loads of water
and plastic sheeting.
The time to cancel debts
was never nearer:
the need for just trade,
never more compelling.
As words come back to us
may they be words of hope
that change lives
and nurture justice.

© Janet Lees

Extracts from the speech given by the Chancellor of the Exchequer, the Rt Hon Gordon Brown at CAFOD's Pope Paul VI Memorial Lecture, December 2004

(some of which was reflected in his speech when he launched the UK Campaign for a Marshall Plan for Africa)

… it is the churches and faith groups that have, across the world, done more than any others – by precept and by example – to make us aware of the sheer scale of human suffering – and our duty to end it.

… when the history of the crusade against global poverty is written, one of its first and finest chapters will detail the commitment of the churches in Britain to help the world's poor.

… we are not powerless individuals but, acting together, have the power to shape history.

… we know that a quarter of all child deaths can be prevented if children sleep beneath bed-nets costing only 4 dollars each.

… the world knows all too well that we have not done enough. Because what is lacking is will.

… lives in the poorest countries depend upon converting, in the richest countries, apathy to engagement, sympathy to campaigning, half hearted concern to wholly committed action.

… our dependence upon each other should awaken our consciences to the needs not just of neighbours but of strangers;

… the globalisation we are witnessing asks us to open our minds to the plight and the pain of millions we will never meet and are continents away but upon whom, as a result of the international division of labour, we depend upon for our food, our clothes, our livelihoods, our security.

… we are in an era of global interdependence, relying each upon the other – a world society of shared needs, common interests, mutual responsibilities, linked densities, our international solidarity.

… we have obligations to others beyond our front doors and garden gates, responsibilities to others beyond the city wall, duties to others beyond our national borders … we are called to answer the hunger of the hungry, the needs of the needy the suffering of the sick whoever and wherever they are … we cannot be fully human unless we care about the dignity of every human being.

… if the dignity of a child or adult is diminished by poverty, or debt, or unfair trade, we are all diminished.

… fair trade is not just about the financial gains, its also about giving people dignity – enabling people to stand on their own two feet and using trade as a springboard out of poverty.

… if we could with all the power at our command, working together, collectively change the common sense of the age so that people saw that poverty was preventable, should be prevented and then had to be prevented, so that we met the Millennium Development Goals not in 2150 but in 2015, then all else we do in our lives would pale into insignificance and every effort would be worth it.

Is It too Much to Ask?

Is it too much to ask for your blessing?
Not on us, for our need is beyond us
Crouched on this parched ground
Gathering meagre wild plants
And watching hunger stalk.
We invoke your blessing on others.

Surely we can ask your blessing –
Not on our neighbours, for they are dying
With withering crops that once bolstered income
But now are the only stay
For unemployed people.
We invoke your blessing on others.

Can we weep for your blessing?
Not on the rural poor
The smallholders and landless
Dispossessed and displaced
For cheap trade.
We invoke your blessing on others.

Shall we die for your blessing?

Not on our governments
Losing power and control
Watching their people emptied
By structural adjustment programmes.
We invoke your blessing on others.

We are trampled for your blessing.
On these: on the faceless and stony
Shareholders and movers
Trans-national corporations
Pushing to harness this world.
We invoke your blessing on these.

Open their souls to daylight
Awaken their eyes to knowledge
Enliven their ears to follow the strain
Of the call for justice
From those who know not
The words of peace and life.
We invoke your blessing on these.
Then may we all be blessed.

© Duncan L. Tuck

Die to Our Greed

The fairness of God shows the justice of giving
a share to each one, from the world and its store,
and then, in this sharing, that we find disturbing,
no-one will be homeless, no-one will be poor.

Extravagant sacrifice, utter self giving;
outrageous the call on what we have to give:
to bring in the justice of God through our living,
then die to our greed, that our neighbours might live.

Our trade and our lives must be fair, not a token;
as open as Christ to each person in need;
as loving as God to the hungry, the broken.
God's spirit brings fruit, where our love plants the seed.

Tune: Streets of Laredo

© Andrew Pratt

Fairly Chocolatey

In the UK chocolate is very popular – and it's not exactly hard to get us to eat even more. Hardly surprising, then, that a new sort of chocolate was one of the first truly fair trade items to hit the market. Let me take you through the process, bean to bar …

The magical ingredient in chocolate is the cocoa. This starts off in a pod on the theobroma cacao, or cacao tree (pronounced kakow). These pods are about the size of rugby balls, and can weigh up to a kilogram. Ripe cacao pods come in a variety of colours; red, green, orange, purple. The word cacao comes from the Latin name of the tree on which the pods grow, and is used until the beans have been fermented, dried and are ready for shipping. Only after this stage are they described as cocoa. When cut open the pod reveals up to forty-five beans surrounded by a white pulp, all of which is carefully removed by hand. The pulp and beans are

© Eric Boa

placed in wooden boxes lined with banana leaves, covered with more leaves and left to ferment for about five days. This kills the beans and breaks down the sugars, as well as beginning to develop the fine flavours. After this the beans are spread on mats to dry in the sun. In good weather this will usually take about a week. This means they will not rot during storage and take on a hard, shrunken and dark to medium brown appearance.

On arrival at the factory the beans are de-stoned and cleaned. An intense blast of heat is fired at them to loosen the shells from the inside nibs. The shells are then forced open to release the nibs. Once removed from the beans the nibs are roasted at over one hundred degrees centigrade to develop the rich flavour and colour of cocoa. The roasted nibs are ground up to produce cocoa mass, which is made up of cocoa particles in fifty to fifty-five percent cocoa butter. This cocoa mass is made into chocolate by further processing and the addition of extra ingredients. It can also be separated to make cocoa powder and cocoa butter. After this the chocolate is passed through rollers and a conching stage, which involves stirring the chocolate while keeping it at a controlled temperature. These last stages are essential in producing smooth chocolate with good flavour.

This chocolate then goes into the shops, where what we buy makes a difference to people thousands of miles away. The chairman of the cooperative that produces the beans for the story that I have been following once said that when you buy a bar of fair trade chocolate you send a child to school, and it's true – fair trade changes lives for the better.